the wedding singer

The Musical Comedy

Photography by Joan Marcus 2006

Piano/vocal arrangements by John Nicholas

Cherry Lane Music Company
Director of Publications/Project Editor: Mark Phillips
Manager of Publications: Gabrielle Fastman

ISBN-13: 978-1-57560-935-5

Visit our website at www.cherrylane.com

"It's Your Wedding Day"

"A Note from Linda"

"Pop!"

"Somebody Kill Me"

"A Note from Grandma"

"Come Out of the Dumpster"

"Saturday Night in the City"

"All About the Green"

"Single"

"If I Told You"

Stephen Lynch and Company

"Grow Old with You"

contents

synopsis

Act One:

It's 1985 and New Jersey's favorite wedding singer, Robbie Hart, is rocking the reception hall with his signature tune, IT'S YOUR WEDDING DAY. When Robbie's band takes a break, he bumps into the new waitress, Julia Sullivan. It's Julia's first night and she can't help imaging what it would be like if she were the bride. She's sure it's bound to happen SOMEDAY.

The following day, Robbie gets ready for his own wedding with the help of his Grandma Rosie. But while Robbie's standing at the altar, he receives A NOTE FROM LINDA. It seems that Robbie's fiancée has changed her mind. Robbie is devastated.

Meanwhile, in the bathroom of the banquet hall, Julia is preparing for a date with her boyfriend, Glen. Her cousin Holly and her mother, Angie, try to convince her that Glen's going to propose. The set changes to a tacky revolving restaurant where Glen indeed finally asks Julia to marry him (POP!).

Still a wreck from being dumped, Robbie refuses to leave his bed. Instead, he spends his time writing songs about his now ex-fiancée (SOMEBODY KILL ME). His band mates, Sammy and George, arrive and try to raise his spirits. They give him a letter they find taped to his bedroom door (A NOTE FROM GRANDMA). Convinced he must get back on the horse, Robbie agrees to play another wedding gig. But as soon as he's back at work, his depression turns to rage and he destroys the reception (CASUALTY OF LOVE).

The angry wedding guests toss Robbie into a dumpster outside the hall. Miserable, Robbie refuses to leave until Julia convinces him to COME OUT OF THE DUMPSTER.

Julia suggests that Robbie play non-wedding functions in order to get his feet wet again. Robbie takes her advice and books a bar mitzvah (TODAY YOU ARE A MAN). Robbie then introduces George, the band's keyboard player, saying that he has written a special song for the occasion (GEORGE'S PRAYER). While George sings, Julia tells Robbie that Glen is too busy to help her register for wedding gifts. Robbie reluctantly agrees to stand in for Glen. As they make their way through the Ridgefield Galleria, Robbie and Julia constantly get mistaken for a couple (NOT THAT KIND OF THING).

Julia and Robbie meet up with Holly at the bridal salon. Holly demands to know what Julia's wedding kiss will be like. After some cajoling from Holly, Julia practices the kiss on Robbie. Sparks fly. Never having seen this side of Robbie, Holly decides to ask him out on a date.

In fact, everyone gets stoked for a SATURDAY NIGHT IN THE CITY. At the club, Holly realizes that Robbie has fallen for Julia. She tells him that Julia is marrying Glen because he's rich. Robbie vows to become more like Glen to win Julia over as the curtain falls.

Act Two:

Determined to start making money, Robbie shows up on Wall Street and asks Glen for a job. Glen reinforces Robbie's suspicions that life is truly ALL ABOUT THE GREEN.

Meanwhile, Julia grills Holly about what happened at the club. Holly admits that she kissed Robbie, but nothing happened. Sammy shows up and tries to put the moves on Holly. Holly blows him off but can't deny that she's starting to have feelings for him (RIGHT IN FRONT OF YOUR EYES).

Julia finds out that Robbie has quit the band and is now working on Wall Street. She confronts Robbie, telling him he can't give up his music. Robbie tells Julia that she's marrying Glen only because he's got money. Julia storms off and Robbie goes to a bar to drink his problems away.

Sammy and George show up and find Robbie getting drunk. They try to cheer him up by singing the joys of being SINGLE. The song only makes Robbie decide to tell Julia how he really feels. Robbie arrives at Julia's house and sees her through her window, dressed in her wedding gown. Afraid she'll reject him, he decides not to tell her he's in love with her (IF I TOLD YOU).

Drunk and depressed, Robbie arrives home to find Linda waiting for him. She tries to restart their relationship, but Robbie ends up passing out (LET ME COME HOME).

Julia shows up the next morning and finds Linda in Robbie's bedroom. Thinking they are back together, Julia decides to elope with Glen to Vegas.

Robbie arrives at an anniversary party for his grandparents and Holly tells him that Julia and Glen have eloped. He decides to go after them. George and Rosie are left onstage alone. They provide their own style of music for the party (MOVE THAT THANG).

Robbie arrives in Vegas but can't find Julia and Glen. He meets up with a few celebrity impersonators who help him locate the missing couple. Robbie crashes the wedding and sings Julia his latest composition (GROW OLD WITH YOU). Robbie proposes and Julia accepts. The happy couple, along with the Vegas impersonators, head home to Jersey. The show ends at Robbie and Julia's wedding reception (IT'S YOUR WEDDING DAY).

CHAD BEGUELIN

Chad Beguelin wrote the lyrics and co-wrote the book for *The Wedding Singer* (Tony Award Nomination for Best Book and Best Original Score, Drama Desk Award Nomination for Outstanding Lyrics). He also wrote the book and lyrics for *The Rhythm Club* (Signature Theater) and *Wicked City* (American Stage Company, Mason Street Warehouse), and wrote the book for Disney's stage version of *Aladdin* (Hyperion Theater). He is the recipient of the Edward Kleban Award for Outstanding Lyric Writing, the Jonathan Larson Performing Arts Foundation Award, and the Gilman & Gonzalez-Falla Musical Theater Award. His plays have been produced at Playwrights Horizon, the Avalon Theatre Company, and HOME for Contemporary Theatre and Art.

MATTHEW SKLAR

Matthew Sklar composed the music for *The Wedding Singer* (Tony Award nomination for Best Original Score and a Drama Desk Award nomination for Outstanding Music). He also co-produced the show's cast album for Sony/BMG Masterworks Broadway. Matthew is a recipient of the Gilman & Gonzalez-Falla Musical Theater Award and the Jonathan Larson Performing Arts Foundation Award. His original musicals include *The Rhythm Club* (Signature Theater), *Wicked City* (American Stage Company, Mason Street Warehouse), and various projects for Disney. Since the age of 18, Matthew has worked extensively on Broadway as a pianist and conductor for a dozen productions, including *Caroline, or Change; Nine; 42nd Street; Titanic; Miss Saigon; and Les Misérables.*

It's Your Wedding Day

Lyrics by
Chad Beguelin

Music by
Matthew Sklar

9

and I are in de- mand.___ And now, cou- ples all o-

ver Jer- sey hi- re me to in- sure ___ their wed- ded bliss, ___

___ all be- cause of a tune ___ I wrote. That tune ___ goes like ___

this: Oh, when it's your wed- ding day ___

Robbie, Sammy & George: So, when it's your wed- ding day ___

and my mu - sic starts ___ to play, ___ I can
and my mu - sic starts ___ to play, ___ I can

guar - an - tee ___ that *All:* love will find ___ you.
guar - an - tee ___ that *All:* love will find ___ you.

Robbie: Yeah, when it's your wed - ding day, ___ all the prob-
Robbie, Sammy & George: Yeah, when it's your wed - ding day, ___ all the prob -

lems melt ___ a - way ___ if you count ___ on me, ___ 'cause
lems melt ___ a - way ___ if you count ___ on me, ___ 'cause

We might play you some "Care - less Whis - per"   or make you wish you had

Sammy & George:

All: "Jes - sie's Girl" ___ in - stead. ___   *Sammy & George:* Bring the room down with "End -

D.S. al Coda

less Love," __ then blast ___ "Bang Your Head." _ *All:* "Bang Your Head"!

Robbie:

Tacet

Coda

do. _____   *Robbie:* And long be - fore __ the night _

sim.

Someday

Lyrics by
Chad Beguelin

Music by
Matthew Sklar

(Spoken:) "Did you see the bride? She looks so perfect." "I know.

Don't you hate her?" "Hate her? She's so happy!"

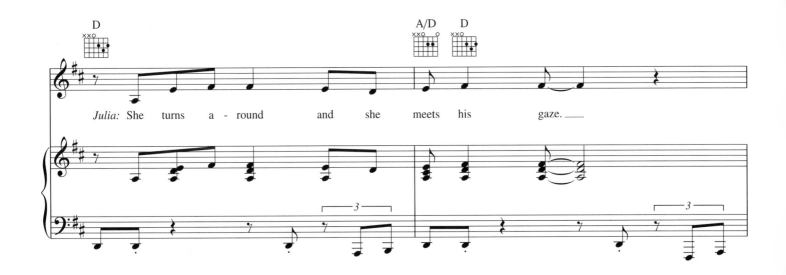

Julia: She turns a - round and she meets his gaze. ___

I know not ev - 'ry mar - riage lasts

when things ___ go bad. ___

I've seen the warn - ing signs; ___ I

call them "mom and dad." ___

A Note from Linda

Lyrics by
Chad Beguelin

Music by
Matthew Sklar

Moderately slow, softly (à la Pachelbel's Canon)

Linda: To my dear-est Rob-bie, I think we need some space.

Please for-give my tim-ing. Dot, dot, dot, smil-ey face. ___ You

see, I woke this morn-ing pre-pared to walk on air but

real-ized ___ that you cramped my style as I crimped my ___ hair. You're

just not that same per-son, the guy I used to know. ___ I'm

not in love ___ with Rob-bie now ___ but Rob-bie sev-en years _____ a - go. ___

Hard Rock feel

You could have been in Möt - ley Crüe ___ or

so it's best ___ we end this be - fore we ___ e - ven

start. Signed, your pal, Lin - da. The

"i" is dot - ted with a bro - ken heart. ___

Pop!

Lyrics by
Chad Beguelin

Music by
Matthew Sklar

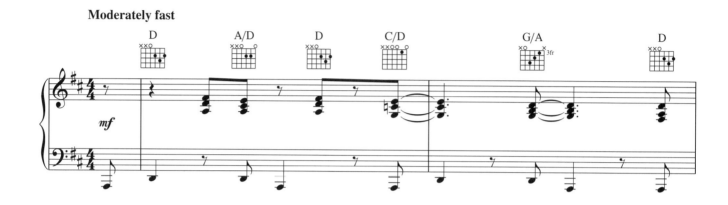

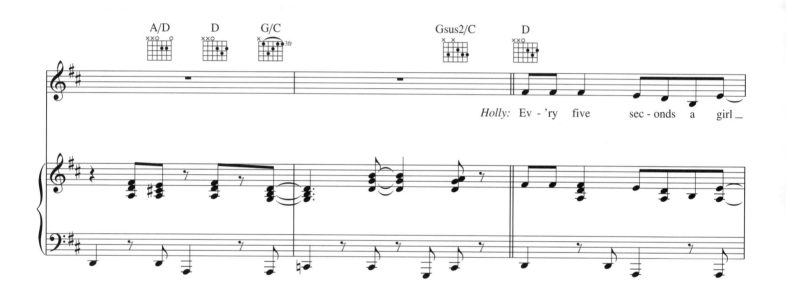

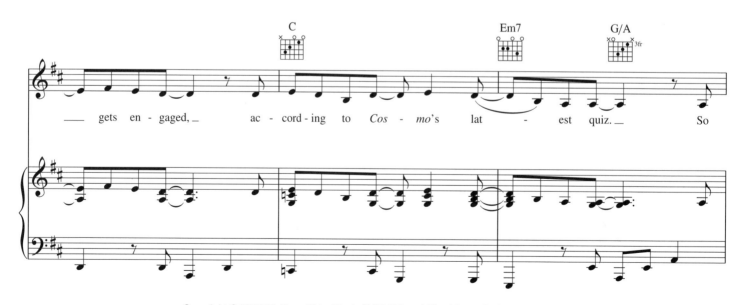

ev - 'ry five sec - onds you get ____ one more chance ____ to make him get down ____ on that knee ____

____ of ____ his. ____ It's a chal - lenge that ev - 'ry wom - an fac - es, so

let's make sure ____ that we've cov - ered our bas - es. *Angie:* You've lived off Tab and Lean Cui - sine, con - *Holly:*

cealed your flaws with May - bel - line. *Both:* You're mint - y fresh and zest - ful - ly clean.

37

place is now so crys - tal clear. Like our re - la - tion - ship, we're
gaged or I hear one more cork, it's ha - ri - ka - ri with this

go - ing 'round in cir - cles here. And where he's sit - ting, it's as
fan - cy lit - tle sal - ad fork. He nixed the bub - bly, which can

if it all re - volves a - round him.
on - ly mean the out - look is grim.

All: He to - tal - ly

popped   the ques - tion, to - tal - ly   popped   the ques-

tion. _____ So there's no rea-son to stop and ques-tion his love. _____

Guys: Ques-tion his love. _____

Girls: Ques-tion his love. ____

Tacet

(Spoken:) Glen: What do you say? Julie: Yes!

All: His love! _____

Somebody Kill Me

Music and Lyrics by
Adam Sandler and Tim Herlihy

Moderately fast

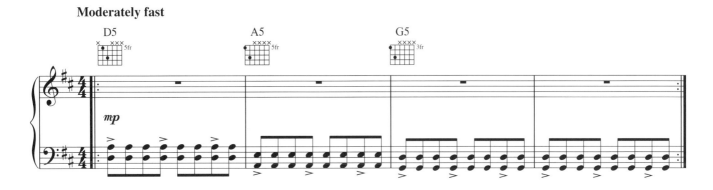

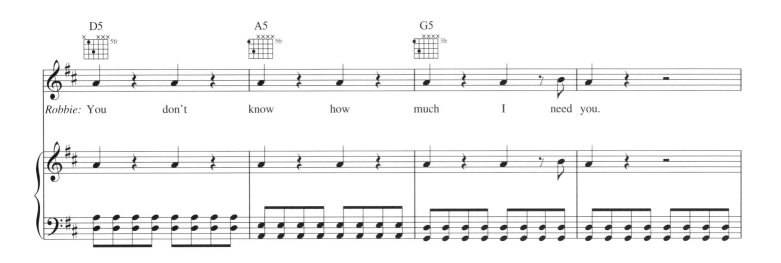

Robbie: You don't know how much I need you.

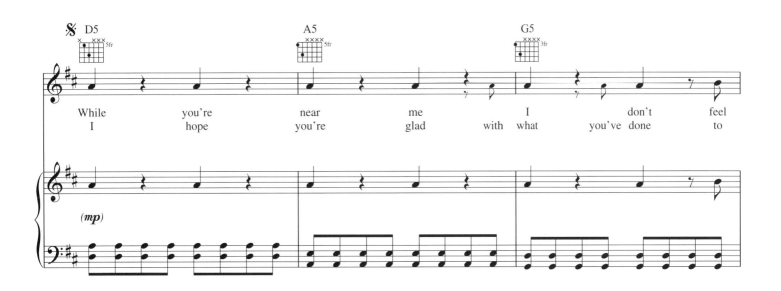

While you're near me I don't feel
I hope you're glad with what you've done to

41

A Note from Grandma

Lyrics by
Chad Beguelin

Music by
Matthew Sklar

Rosie: To my dear-est Rob-bie, I know you're feel-ing low. And

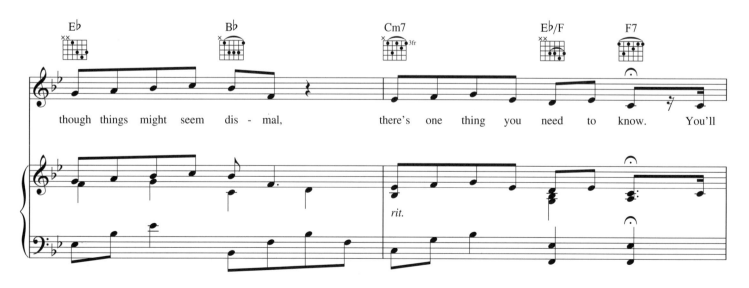

though things might seem dis-mal, there's one thing you need to know. You'll

find some-one who loves you, sure as waves will find the shore. And

when you're sad, re-mem - ber that

Lin - da is a skank - y whore.

Come Out of the Dumpster

Lyrics by
Chad Beguelin

Music by
Matthew Sklar

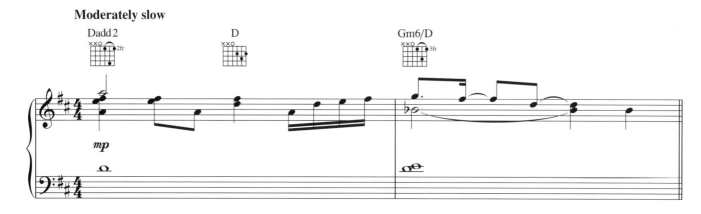

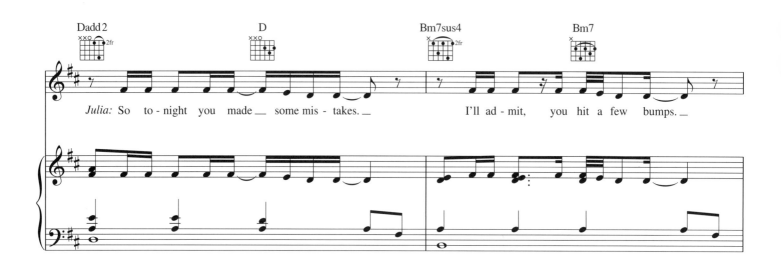

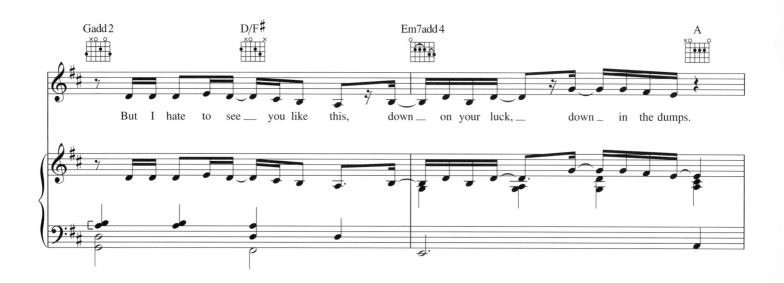

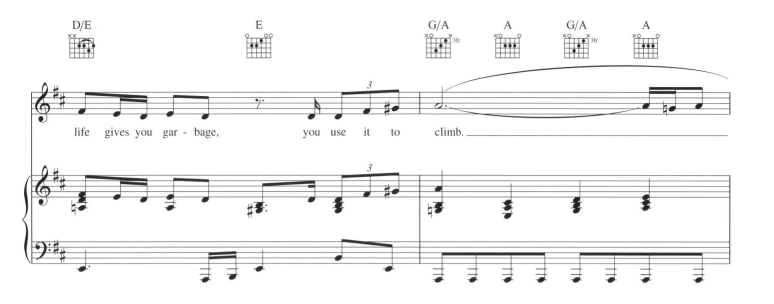

life gives you gar - bage, you use it to climb. _____

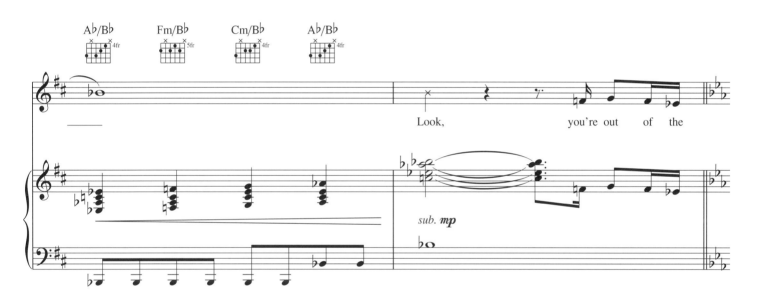

_____ Look, you're out of the

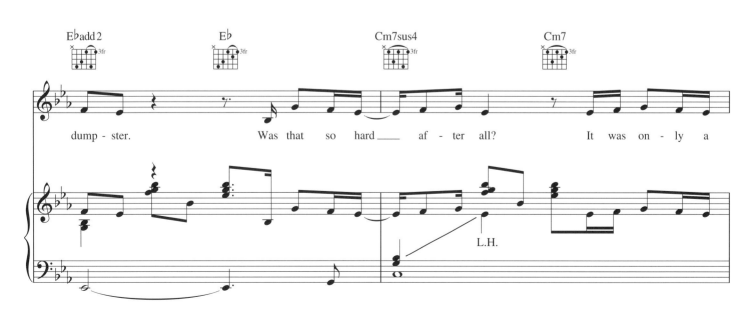

dump - ster. Was that so hard____ af - ter all? It was on - ly a

Not That Kind of Thing

Lyrics by
Chad Beguelin

Music by
Matthew Sklar

53

when her eyes ____ meet mine ____ and lin - ger there ____

may - be a bit ____ too long. ____

Julia: And ____ I won - der ____ is ____ there some -

thing hid - den in ____ his stare? ____

No, I could-n't be _____ more wrong! _____

All: Tell _____ the _____ night _____ to save _____ its _____ moon - light.

Tell _____ the _____ birds _____ not _____ to _____ sing. _____

Tell _____ the _____ stars _____ in _____ the _____ heav - ens _____ they've _____ been _____

Saturday Night in the City

Lyrics by
Chad Beguelin

Music by
Matthew Sklar

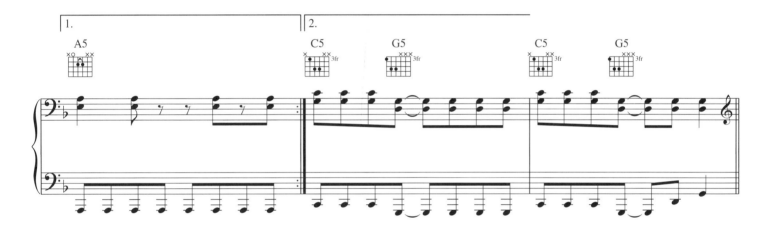

wild - est dreams ___ come true. *Julia:* The dance ___ floor smoke, ___ *Glen:* a bump ___

___ of coke, ___ *George:* and ev - 'ry - thing ___ ta - boo. ___

Robbie: I got a pair of par - a - chute pants that Grand - ma bought me to wear. ___

___ *Sammy:* Can't wait ___ till chicks ___ start flock - ing to ___ my Flock ___

All: Whoa, oh, oh, oh. Whoa, oh, oh. Sat - ur - day night _ in the cit - y. _____

Sat - ur - day night ___ in the cit - - y. _____
Whoa, oh, oh, oh, _____ oh. _____

mp

All About the Green

Lyrics by
Chad Beguelin

Music by
Matthew Sklar

green.   It's all a-bout the green.___

Some may say you're head-ed down a ___ crook-ed trail, ___ but

if you sell your soul, at least you made a sale.___

You could end world hun-ger or cre-ate a vac-cine,___ but if you

buy - ing out the Jap - a - nese. Land deals down in Bo - ca. Do - ing drinks with I - a - coc - ca.

Yeah, it's all a - bout the green.
Wan - na be some - bod - y?
It's all a - bout the

green. _____
Wan - na be some - bod - y?
It's all a - bout the...

green. _____ Wan - na be some - bod - y? It's all a - bout the...

Cor - p'rate hacks like stab - bing backs _ and twist - ing arms _ real slow. _

But you on - ly hol - ler un - cle if _____ your un -

cle is the C - E - O. _____ Yeah, it's all a - bout the

Yeah, it's all a - bout the green.

All: Wan - na be some - bod - y?

It's all a - bout the

green. _____ Wan - na be some - bod - y?

It's all a - bout the...

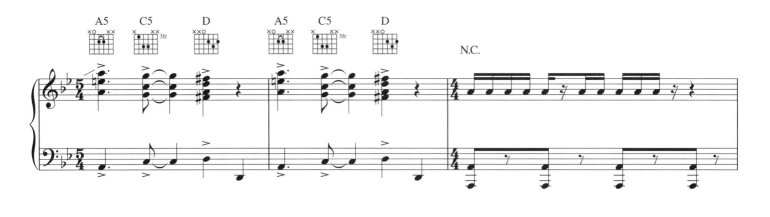

Right in Front of Your Eyes

Lyrics by
Chad Beguelin

Music by
Matthew Sklar

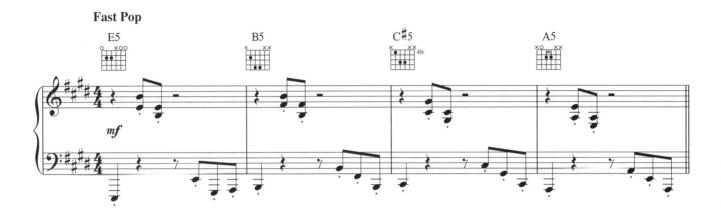

Holly: Ev-'ry time you see his face you get an-noyed. ___
Ev-'ry night a hun-dred guys come through the door. ___

And if ig-no-rance is bliss, he's o-ver-joyed. ___
They take your breath a-way each time they take the floor. ___

wake up one __ day and re - al - ize __ the one __ that you want

is right in front of your eyes? __

You might have a cham - pagne wish __ or two __

Single

Lyrics by
Chad Beguelin

Music by
Matthew Sklar

Moderately fast R&B

Sammy: No one tells ___ you how you

ought to ___ live. ___ No one glares ___ when you do Jell - O ___ shoot - ers.

start the par - ty, start a tab, 'cause you're

sin - gle. You ___ are sin - gle, and you'll

keep stay - in' sin - gle if ___ you're smart. *(Guys:* If you are Yeah, you're

sin - gle, you ___ are sin - gle. No
smart.) _____

chick will ev - er moon - walk on ___ your heart. ___
(*Guys:* Moon - walk on your heart.)

Trust me, this is when the good times real - ly start.

Instrumental...

blast - ing Cher or Wham! _ (Guys: Cher _ or Wham!) _ All: So

fill your Rang - ers cup. The toi - let seat _ stays up. The

fridge gets stocked with beer and Spam, 'cause you're sin - gle. You _ are

George:

sin - gle. _____ Not a care in the world _ can both - er

103

you.
(*Guys:* Can both - er you.) _____

You are sin - gle. You __ are sin - gle. __ You can

do what you've al - ways want - ed to. __ *Well,*
(Al - ways want - ed to.)

no com - mit - ments *All:* 'cause you're on - ly pass - ing

through! *Ricky: Yo!*

Mak - in' a date with some need - y girl __ is a

104

start - ing to see __ where you're com - in' from. __   'Cause I'm

sin - gle. Oh, _____ yeah, sin - gle.   I'll be -

have like a dude's __ meant to __ be - have.   Al - ways

(*Guys:* Meant to be -

sin - gle, ev - er sin - gle.   Sin - gle

have.)

If I Told You

Lyrics by
Chad Beguelin

Music by
Matthew Sklar

ter not to know? ___

Julia: Who's that girl with the per - fect fu - ture? Her re - flec - tion says ___

___ it all. ___ Try - ing hard to pre - tend she's ea - ger,

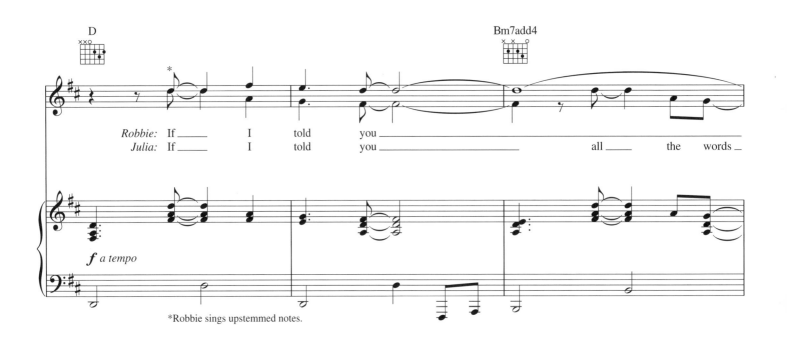

*Robbie sings upstemmed notes.

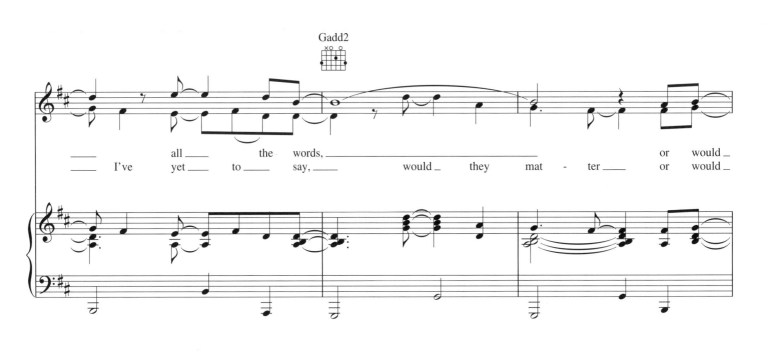

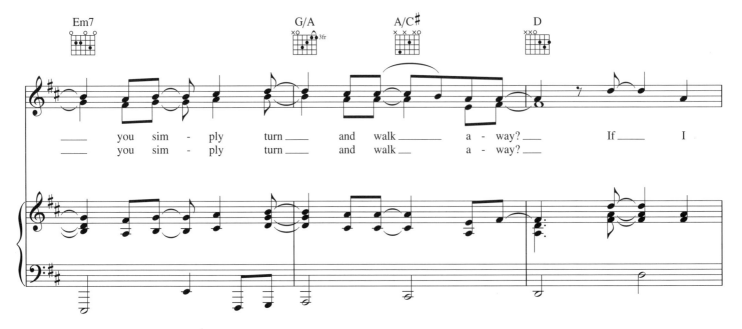

hold you, ___ will ___ you tell ___ me I ___ should go? ___

If ___ I hold ___ you. _____

*Robbie sings downstemmed notes.

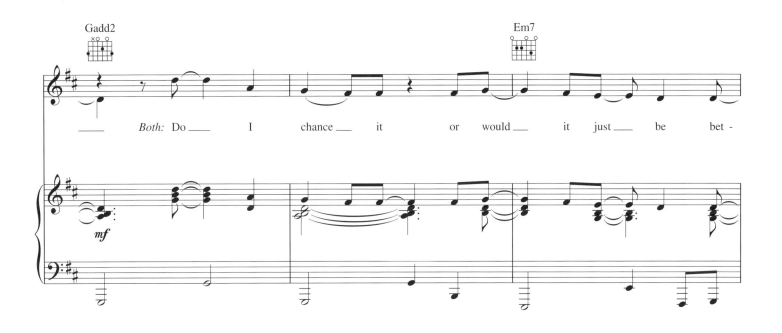

___ *Both:* Do ___ I chance ___ it or would ___ it just ___ be bet -

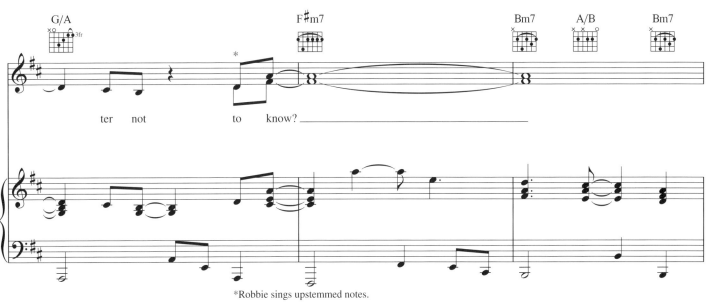

ter not to know? _____

*Robbie sings upstemmed notes.

*Robbie sings upstemmed notes.

Let Me Come Home

Lyrics by
Chad Beguelin

Music by
Matthew Sklar

Moderate Rock

Linda: I know I kind of went out with a bang _ when I dumped you out of the blue. _

_ But my heart's just like a

boom-er-ang; _ it came right back to you. _ Now

mor - row when you wake _ up, you'll no long - er have an ex, ___ 'cause the best _

___ part of a break - up is the make - up sex. ___

Let me come home ___ to you, ba - by. Let me come

Grow Old with You

Music and Lyrics by
Adam Sandler and Tim Herlihy

Robbie: I wan-na make you smile whe-ev-er you're sad, __

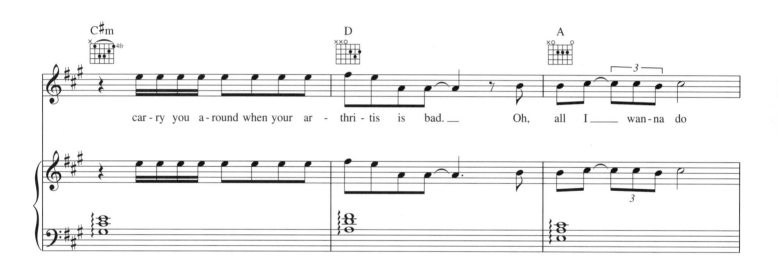

car-ry you a-round when your ar-thri-tis is bad. __ Oh, all I __ wan-na do

is grow old with you. I'll get your

e - ven let you hold the re - mote con - trol. __ So let me do the dish - es in our __

__ kitch - en sink, _ put you to bed __ when you've had too __ much to drink. _ Oh,

I could be the man __ who grows old with you.

Robbie, Julia: I'll miss you, __ kiss you, __ take your shoes off and

*Robbie sings upper part.

126

More Great Piano/Vocal Books

FROM CHERRY LANE

For a complete listing of Cherry Lane titles available,
including contents listings, please visit our web site at
www.cherrylane.com

See your local music dealer or contact:

CHERRY LANE
MUSIC COMPANY
6 East 32nd Street, New York, NY 10016

Quality in Printed Music

EXCLUSIVELY DISTRIBUTED BY

HAL•LEONARD®
CORPORATION
7777 W. BLUEMOUND RD. P.O. BOX 13819 Milwaukee, WI 53213

Prices, contents and availability subject to change without notice.
0404